The
Despairationist

These are not words, they are tears.

Mohammed
Ahmed

@style_poet

<u>Acknowledgements</u>

Thank you to my mother and father.
For always being there. Dad your pep talks are phenomenal.
And Mum, no words can express, you are simply amazing.

Best wishes to those who hurt me.
Kindest Regards to those who healed me.
It's a part of life.
Some people teach you a lesson,
Whilst others stand by you.

A special thank you to Humaira.
Words cannot portray the gratitude I feel
towards you for the support and motivation.

<u>Special Message on Page 101</u>

Contents

Love

What is love I asked myself obliviously?
I had just been rejected by the girl whom I loved
limitlessly.

Is love the foundation of destruction
or reincarnation of life?
Either way, I figured you found someone to call
your husband or wife.
Would you be forced into a commitment or would
you establish your own fraternity?
I just hoped with God's grace I found someone I
could love for an eternity.

Was love an actual bond or just a reason to
implement restrictions?
My opinion in relation to commitments always led
to
disagreements and contradictions.

Will I ever find someone who will leave me
breathless?
I doubted myself because when I saw a girl
I was only left speechless.
My heart never skipped a beat
or felt that aura of different or uniqueness.

But the most significant subject of all kept
pestering
me asked what does love feel like?
Is it an eternity of experiences or a special
sensational connection with that special someone?
Was it the unity of two different lives in order
to fulfill promises or fulfill everlasting desires?

I soon discovered the answers;
the reality of life was it was painful to love.
It was saddening to be aware,
but maybe it was a sign from above?

Love is a complex feeling that some confuse with
lust.
So is love just love or lost, to begin with?
Some believe love develops over time
and this is why there are arranged marriages.

Isn't love supposed to be special or at first sight?

I thought love was to be continued...

Last time

This was the last time I ever saw hope.
She was beautiful and perfect in every way.
It was hard to imagine it would happen this way.

All I ever did was pray.
For one thing that was impossible.

Hope was a breath of fresh air,
Glistening, mesmerizing, a one of one.
Forever changing my life,
an uncomfortable acquaintance.
Now I am left abjured by the memories of her.
Yearning for someone attention by the ever-
contradicting world.

She gave me a key but left a hole.
She was a thief but gave me the gold.
She was a jigsaw, yet I am the one in pieces.

Loveless

I feel like a ghost town, grey as the clouds,
lifeless like a pile of brown fallen leaves
in the winter autumn.
All alone once the sun sets as
I motionlessly wave goodbye to my shadow
-and go through window pain.

Lately, the wind and I have stopped
whistling like we used to,
as a duet, now a divorced couple.
We stick to ourselves,
alone as the night and day.

Lately, the trees and I have stopped
waving at each other like we used to.
Once neighbours, now we stand
across from each other like strangers.

I am dead inside, a deserted forgotten grave no one

remembers.

A dark cloud full of tears and sorrows but no one cares.

A speck of dust that has been wiped off the slate,

Like the corpses of the dead left to rot and disintegrate.

Is this the end?

My screams echoed the empty halls
of an abandoned flat
alike my torn blood vessels.
My blood like a football crowd
slowly covering the blood beneath me.
My shadow a reminiscent of a child playing hangman.
My body a ragdoll,
like clothes hung to dry on a clothesline.

Flashbacks scar my eyes as I blink,
my eyes ambushed by a swarm of people from the press.
Slowly I question whether it was a dream or real,

only to break once again to discover
I was a frozen fish stuck to my mattress.

It was a beautiful nightmare.
I was afraid to live.
So I slept to die.
Hoping dreams transformed into reality
or reality became a dream.

Sleeping in a bath of sweat
and dreaming of death was my game
and I somehow had convinced myself to love playing
it.

I was a predator searching for death;
Nights had become a witch hunt.

Day and night

Every night was worse than the last,
A repressed memory from the past,
Every night was a new experience,
The very reason I spat my existence,
Every night I cried as the light dimmed,
As the darkness mocked me and rose,
Every night I chocked on my own saliva,
It was better than living another day in this life.

Calling it life was perhaps an over-exaggeration, like comparing heaven and hell,
Every day was the life of a vampire cowering from the sunlight,
The light was a fake messenger, a trauma of false hope,
Every day was another war, a day in the trenches,
Fighting for another breath, fighting temptations of suicide,
Every day was perhaps an understatement; every minute was like a year,
Every second was a cry for help like the battle cry of a leader being massacred before his troops.

<u>Oh are you pleased?</u>

Oh.' can you hear my heart, it's on fire,
Oh' you may not know, but you are its desire,
Oh' I'm sorry too because I've gone clinically insane,
Oh' it's a disaster but of all your cocaine.

Oh' have you read the news I'm thirsty for your love,
Oh' did you hear the knocking last night it was my
heart searching for your affection,
Oh' did you smell the smoke in the kitchen it was the
boiling of my blood,
Oh' can you see feel the absence I've disintegrated
awaiting your return.

Oh' have you seen my shadow it was reported missing
since your departure,
Oh' did you hear the smoke alarm because it stopped
singing your departure,
Oh' have you seen my eyes I'm left blinded by your
love,
Oh' did you traumatise my tongue as I'm left
speechless by your love.

Oh' now you need me, so you resurrect my being from my grave,

Oh' you say I should be grateful, then degrade my very being to a slave,

Oh' you chant bitch so much, my self-esteem has deteriorated to the tip of an icicle,

Oh' you say it is all a part of the plan, but day-to-day life is like a rotation on a bicycle.

Oh' did you hear the heavy rain last night It was a pathetic fallacy of my emotions,

Oh' did you see the eclipse that happened It was my heart going black,

Oh' did you see the blood in the sink it's all that's left of me after I left this world.

Oh' did you forget something, of course, your trademark collar

For once I can speak my mind and not have to start with Oh' and be only valued a dollar

Finally free from this fantasy world of yours
- Dead and Gone!

Light conscience

Like an Alzheimer's patient, I was lost for words.
I was left speechless and had nothing but me and my
heart.
Feeling like a criminal about to be interrogated I
wanted to just be honest with myself and my
conscience. So if anything went wrong, I could die an
honest death.
I was over-reacting like a child telling tales. It was like a
fart in a hurricane.

Why are you so honest? She asked me.
I told her I have nothing to lose. What do I have to be
scared of, to tell the truth?
Why are you so humble? She asked me.
I told her it is the only thing the world has not been to
me; I wanted to be different, am I right in think in such
a way?
Why are you so giving? Why does your heart keep
giving? She asked me
I told her, I am heartless; my heart was stolen years
back and given back in pieces.
What do you see in the world?

There was nothing I could say to lighten the blow.

We were opposite sides of the spectrum.

I was the inferno and she was the waterfall, It was impossible, an eclipse that would tarnish the laws of physics.

Second thoughts

Staring into the black abyss of my demise, milliseconds from fate sealed actions.

Everlastingly depriving and changing the lives of those who have my unfortunate acquaintance.

Within in an inch of eternal self-affliction,

Soon to be a transparent soul exiled from the miseries of this world.

There I was milliseconds from unchangeable actions.

Questioning whether it was a dream or reality.

Mind conflicted like the war, ears buzzing with static like a lost cause.

Time running out and the darkness around me like a secret garden.

I was my own stranger, trying to break free from the
bars of my own prison.
I was suddenly filled with empathy, like a phoenix
reborn.
There was nothing left for me in this world
I swallowed my pride and let the fire die.

This was not going to be the death of me, it was never
too late.
These scars would haunt me and the echoes would
daunt me, but it was my fate.
I was my own hero, fighting to live another day in hell,
fight another war.

Dream of hope

And there I saw a transparent devoted soul free from the sorrows and pain of the world.

It could not have been at a better time, place or location.

It almost thrilled and excited my very core; I could sense the fear, the intensity, and the pressure.

Even a stranger passing by you were a heaven of its own kind,

You rekindled a fire in my abyss and hoped it was my time,

And there you were eyes blue and mysterious like the deepest ocean.

You resurrected my last dying heartbeat I was left mystified,

A divine nature with smooth silky wavy black hair,

 A thought so shy I was left startled,

A feeling so luxurious,

I was left speechless and complacent,

A smile so pristine and pure,

It sparked and ignited my heart beat and simulated the blood in my veins,

Those cute dimples on your cheekbones when you
laughed,
I wanted it to last an eternity so I could feel its eternal
warmth,
A breath so intoxicating, it quenched the thirst of my
soul,
A stare so deep, I was entered into an eternal trance,
A heartbeat so synced, it uplifted my spirits,

This could only be, this had always been and ever was,
It was a dream, my last will.
A dying wish, the touch of you was so sensual,
I have disintegrated and await your return.

Just a word

I am just another word,

Another faceless, race less and nameless tick on the register,

Nor remembered, honored or disputed,

Nothing can satiate this heartache, not even love of affection,

Nowadays not even the thought of love can give me satisfaction,

As I sit down and write this I think where in the world my heart will get some good reception.

After all, I am just another one who has come and gone,

As the seconds pass, hours fly and days run I slowly dysfunction,

I am going insane, the signs of life fade and I can no longer function,

I freeze trapped in my maze of eternal disconnection.

A silhouette I waste away, the burning light turning me to ash.

The lonely undignified end is nearing,

The sand beneath my feet is sinking,

An unknown I pass away, my existence fading and my heart-beat dying.

Dead left unburied

Forgotten, unloved and unhurried.

There is nothing left for me in this world.

Have you ever screamed but there was no sound?

Have you ever cried but there were no tears?

Have you ever loved but there was no redemption?

Have you ever wanted to dream, to hope but all you see is darkness when you close your eyes?

This silence is deafening, my thoughts are extinct, and my mind is decaying,

This death is not enough. There is a fault in my stars.

I'm alive but I'm not living, a part of me is dead inside,

Every breath I take is suffocating and intoxicating,

Every thought I have is a worse nightmare than the previous,

Every scream goes unheard alike others,

My heart tortured and stopped beating as the light faded and died out.

Shattered dreams

My journey up to that moment was like a rollercoaster,
-Unpredictable, a thriller that ended in a brutal
massacre,
Its aftermath, smudged make-up, shattered mirrors
and broken horoscopes.
The future as black as the night and in pieces like my
dreams,
A jigsaw puzzle missing pieces and no current solution,
I was now left wandering in the fields of a rubble-filled
abyss of my own creation,
I follow suit and as dawn breaks crumble too, as the
walls around me progressively deteriorate.

When will I have my happy ending? Is it too much to
ask?
As I stare into the empty starless sky and question
destiny, -But nobody is home.
I am a long way from home; I am lost in my thoughts,
I feel numb and warm inside as I witness the glimpses
of heaven, they are only temporary as I imminently
realise the reality of my situation.
In disguise, a beautiful nightmare, every second is
S&M.

<u>Personality</u>

You may not know this but I died once, I mourned my own death as I buried my own self.

I watched as the rain danced on my grave, the shadows laughed and the surroundings rejoiced.

I had no one but myself.

Not even those who wounded me came to save me, unfulfilled promises, and broken relations.

Eternal death ardently awaited my doom.

At that moment in time, everything I was disappeared in a flash, I was in a different dimension far away from here.

All that remained constant was my name, I was just a mystery.

I was just a body.

A vampire filled with despair I roam the streets for a feeling to fill this void,

I am here today writing not from the heart, but my blood, soul, and body.

I always said I am not a quitter, but I am at the pinnacle of my fall,

My strength weakening and I become a nobody.

A series of unfortunate events have shaken the

foundations of my core,
Its repercussions have sent shivers into the deepest
chambers of my heart and left me in the rubble. The
humiliation has awoken a hunger so fierce it
ravenously tears at my flesh and bones.
As the feeling of emptiness slowly fills inside me, I
become lost under the surface.

Being human

Blueblood, purple skin and red eyes,
Were all now the least of my worries.
Shattered dreams, loss of personality and second
thoughts,
Was this all I had to look forward to?

Have you ever looked at the mirror and saw blurred
lines?
Have you ever had second thoughts about taking a
second breath?
Have you ever slept on the shattered glass of your
dreams?

Hope, love and a lighter conscience,
Were all things of my past now.
Disconnection, Despair, and Death,
Was this all I had to look forward to?

Have you ever put your heart on silent because it was
too painful?
How did it make you feel?
Have you ever tried to forget what happened
yesterday?
Even though it was not your fault?
Have you ever tried to run from the past or tried to
escape the inevitable future?
Did anyone care about your feelings?

It's called being human, a broken melody,
So let us sit in circles and now tell me your story.

The message

As I stood and stared at the horizon, I saw a starless sky
filled with nothing but the mist of a storm,
As a cloudy fog began to slowly mass the atmosphere
like the emerging phantom opera,
The leaves performing a grand orchestra without the
guidance of the wind their conductor,
As the grandness of gesture emerged I felt trapped as
the purpose was still unclear.

I could not hear the leaves calling for me,
I could not feel the fog watching out for me,
I could not hear the storm screaming for me,
I could not feel the atmosphere was reaching out to
me.

It was a message from the atmosphere, a safeguard,
The tears of an angel embracing my heart, forever
changing something inside of me,
Mourning the death of a child and rejoicing the rebirth
of a survivor.

I am no longer afraid, even at the darkest hour.

I can finally understand and comprehend the message loud and clear.
I never thought I would exist, never thought I could be.

But something changed inside me,
When the atmosphere called for me,
The darkness embraced me.

The red room

With every breath, it was another moment lost,
With every moment of silence, it was another question raised,
With every wrong answer, it was another cut on my wrists.

Another sleepless night in the red sea, another abstract painting by dawn,
Another nightmare in the pool of death, feeling paralyzed.
Another day terrified of everything I used to love.

With every second, it was the death of another

forgotten memory,

With every hour, it was another thought of death.

With every day, I prayed that it would be the last.

Another hopeless day staring into thin air, another cloud of judgment by night,

Another dream in the dimension of the hereafter, feeling trapped.

Another night terrified of everything I used to love.

There is nothing left for me.

To say, or feel.

Last will

Hanging on a thread, counting the stars,

Fading to black, suffocating as my lungs collapse,

As I deliver apologies for all my indiscretion, forgive me for all I have done.

Wearing my heart on my sleeve, I am so mad at myself for giving in to temptations,

I've tried to be the best I can, but I am not the best of creation,

Pardon me for all I have said, as I am moving on.

Just let the world know I will be okay, I guess; I will be in a better place.

I am not as strong as I used to be, a castle of glass, I am piece one in a million.

Just let the world know I am in a better place,

A phoenix reborn.

I am a butterfly, fragile yet floating, just trying to hang on.

I was told that perfection could be seen in the darkest of places, so I was just changing places.

I needed a torch to light a fire inside of me, so I could see clearly.

But the stars faded, and so did my brain cells.

Transitioning to an Alzheimer's patient everything was anti-matter,

A language I could not speak, a memory I could not remember, and a mind I could not control.

Just let the world know, I found my cure, I found my tourniquet.

I am holding strong, once a broken mirror now a warrior reborn. Just let the world know, I have found salvation.

Disconnected

I am disconnected and far away, a bird who has lost its wings.
The feelings of joy, significance and romance are a thing of the dark disturbing past.

I am trapped in an hourglass of depression plastered with rejection,
I have been exiled by the people of the world, and this is the spell they cast.
I am left broken, my confidence on the brink of extinction and self-esteem thinner than the tip of an icicle.

I am at a standstill, stuck in these dark days with no hope on the horizon.
I am a deserted island with no bridge, a sad ghost with no place to call home.
I am a city who cannot see the sun, a voice that is unheard.

I am disconnected and far away, a clock who has no

moving hands.
The feelings of hope, acceptance, and commitment are
a thing of the dark disturbing past.

Will the feeling of numbness inside me ever
disappear?
Will the insecurities of being alone ever leave me
alone?
Will I ever get away? Or will I be stuck for eternity?

Abnormal

The smoke in my lungs, the poison in my veins,
The longing feeling of disdain that I have inside of me,
The visions in my eyes, the voices in my ears,
The glimpses of hell – the demons that I have around
me,
The scars are hidden deep within my heart,
The weight of the world in my hands,
The addiction of the past, the imaginary friend that
keeps calling for me,
The shackles on my legs,
 I have walked this path for too long,
The guilt overcomes me I choke on the words in my

throat,

The thought of not standing a chance, like an
avalanche, represses me,

Nausea as I inhale the fumes in my nose,

The tears flowing down my cheeks, the ache in my
legs,

I fall down to my knees as I feel myself going under.

There are tears on the ground, broken into pieces with
my pride.

There is blood on my shirt, I am wounded, stolen is my
dignity.

The pain emerges as I scream tearing apart my vocal
chords,

Blood curdles in my throat as I choke and realise my
eventual demise.

My ship is sinking, can anyone respond?

My heart is drowning, can anyone help me
understand?

My world is ending, is there still hope for me?

My sky is falling, is there space for me?

Will you give up on me? Will you save me?

Will you pretend I am not affected?

 Tell me I am normal.

Confessions of a hopeaholic

I say I am ok, but I am not. Keep telling myself I am fine, but I am not.

I try to stay busy, but it is not enough. Keep trying to move on, but it is not enough.

I am just swimming in my own tears, the tears of a clown who masks his own sorrow.

I am not really sure how I feel about it, but there is not much I am able to do.

It is not much of a life I am living; I am just giving not taking.

I have walked this path for far too long, but there is nothing I can do.

And the truth will always haunt me, a feeling I can never escape.

I turn on the lights, but I still see darkness, I just can't hide away.

I feel hopeless, every passing second, like nothing can save me.

It is how I am feeling, a symphony that I play.

Oh no I have said too much.
 I am ok, I will be fine.

Conflict of rejection

In the beginning, it was our home a heaven on its own,
but now it is just a vivid dream.
Love was our connection, but you took it away from
me,
I was your soldier, your protector, your warrior, but
that is all gone, the butterflies along with the time.
I am left drenched, every element of my feelings
dissolved and hopes shattered.
Time passes and seasons change, but you are still the
common denominator.
All that remains on the battlefield.

I wish I could turn back the time, turn over the tide, be
with you,
Just one more time, feel the nectar of your lips on
mine,
Just one more time, smell the perfumes the incense of
your perfection,
I wish I could back the time, turn over the tide, and run
away,
Just one more time, see the color of your rainbow and
see the reflection of your monster.

Just one more time, so I could run away from this
madness before I was in too deep and drowned.

And now I am left with nothing but this disease,
As I scream and curse fate,
For what did you make me fall into this illusion if you
were not the one to reciprocate?
For what do I owe to be gifted this retribution, If you
were not the capable one to invigorate?
For what have I been hit with this storm of love
recession?
I hope you have heard that I have been diagnosed with
depression.

The soiree

Standing at the summit of my demise,

With the certainty that I was not going home after tonight,

With the certainty that reality would be an eclipse, nothing would ever be the same again.

Even after going through it a thousand times, like an imam reciting a prayer,

Even travelling a thousand miles, like a refugee with no place to call home,

It was still not enough to outrun, to escape.

With clouded eyes, a heart of lies and bloodshot eyes I accepted that I could not cheat fate.

I stood no chance, and there was nothing I could do but sleep in the bed of thorns that fate had gifted to me.

I stood no chance, even though I was terminally sick and tired of hiding; I was only running away from something I could never change. Something I could never stop from happening.

Another victim I was immobilised, another one no will ever find out the truth about.

It was just a soiree with my shadow and a couple of ghosts.

<u>When I'm gone</u>

When I am six feet under, do not shed a tear.

When I am six feet under, do not disappear,

When I am six feet under, do not forget our time together all those years.

Just pray for me, just be discrete, and just pray for me.

Please, my dearest, do not shed a tear, it will only make it worse.

It will flaw only my existence, increase our distance and stain our coexistence.

Just close your eyes, remember the time we spent and just pray for me.

Just remember when my wedding, oh it never happened as I ceased to exist.

Please, my dearest, treat it the same,

It never happened, I am not deceased.

I do not want you to cry, we cannot surrender.

Even though our bond is now invisible, our feelings are still mutual.

Just smile like nothing is wrong.

Just pray for me. Just be discrete. And just pray for me.

Love? No comment

I was now an angel with broken wings, nowhere to fly,

A lover on a lonely road with no final destination, at the edge of my world,

Wishing I could be on higher ground, greener grass and a brighter future.

Wishing I could give exile to all these bad things, erase the past, to start over.

I guess it was naivety. I guess I had a lot to learn.

I was now an algebra formulae unsolved, lost in transmission,

A lover looking for love in the wrong place, an unplanned pregnancy,

Wishing I was wiser, that I looked the other way.

Wishing I could pull out in time before

I got too attached before it hurt.

I guess it was it was immaturity. I guess I had a lot to learn.

You always did have a way with words, a magician of conversation,

Your glistening smile, the spark in your eyes,

The purity of your words,

You were my definition of perfection.

You always did have my back, maybe you needed a
place to stab.
Your unexplained meetings, the emptiness in your
blank stares,
Was I your definition of perfection?
Did I ruin it at the cost of my undoubting discretion?
All I ever wanted was your happiness,
Whether it made me happy or sad.

So I ask you.
 What is love?

Have you ever been in love?
Do you know how it feels?
Did you choose to fall in love?
Have you ever had second thoughts?
Did you always believe in love?
Why did you fall in love?
How did you know it was genuine?

I am better now; I can answer each of those without
shedding a tear.

Did you always believe in love?

Would you fall out of love?

No comment.

Issues

In the beginning, it used to be just your story. But now you are my story.

Tell me about your scars and let me change your history.

I may not be able to change your past, but I will be there for your future.

Tell me your secrets and I will tell you all about mine too.

Let us open Pandora's' box and prepare for the worst.

Tell me you won't leave now and I will do the same.

I may not be perfect, but you are my definition of perfection.

And then maybe then I can understand
why you have chosen me.

In the beginning, I was just a mystery, and you knew nothing about my story.

I wanted to let you in but was scared that you would be like the rest.

I would let you in but you would only want out.

I would cry out my heart and you would leave my tears on the runaway.

I would tell you everything and in the end, you would call me abnormal.

I would give you the key to my heart and you would leave it all in pieces.

And then maybe I can understand why I keep choosing you.

It used to be our story, but now we are each other's story.

Tell me about your time and I'll tell you about mine.

Maybe this time will be different.

Bleeding thoughts

My heart bleeds for you, forming red carpets for your
arrival,
My skin pleads for you, thirsting for your very touch,
My mind always thinking of you, every thought starts
first with you,
My eyes blinded and await your return;
they won't set their eyes on anyone else.

My soul it trembles, it has been too long since you have
gone, you are its only hope of survival,
My body you are its cocaine, its addiction, now
seemingly an affliction.

My thoughts conflicted, anxious and indecisive.
What do I mean to you? Where do we stand? Who am
I to you?

My tongue inflicted with disease, it calls for you.
You are its recitation, its dying wish.

You are my drug.

<u>Changes</u>

You changed me.

You made me.

Then you left me.

I wish I could be okay with that.

The day was now my enemy,

There was no hope in sight,

The light drifting away like the shifting sands of a
desert,

As if a drought was upon me,

A calamity was about to unfold,

Destiny revealing the next chapter of my life, a story
untold,

Days passed by like sandstorm winds.

Nights were like frostbite, a day on Everest.

Everest would have been an easier feat but this was an
elusive mission.

An obscurity haunting my dreams, every time a vision
of you,

A collage of our time together, it dug up my scars and
left fresh wounds.

Days were like dreaming with my eyes open,
A museum of me and you.
I was a tourist of my demented own love story.

Wish I could move on, Wish it was that easy.
Wonder if you wonder, wonder if you look back.
Do you ever think of you and me?

I want to know do you think there will be a next time
around.

Broken record

Staring at a dark empty sky searching for the stars,
A shooting a star, to wish for freedom, to forget my
scars,
Reflecting, wondering and questioning how it all went
so wrong?
Remembering our first kiss, missing your soft angelic
touch, dying to say one last goodbye,
If only I could go back in time, to relive the moment
once again.
The nostalgia kills me every time, a fresh gunshot

wound.

But I am just one sad love song, a broken record.

How can I live without my chorus?

What is my serving purpose without my record player?

Who will hear my story?

Who will answer my screams?

Who will share my story?

I guess I was foreseeing my own eventual demented
dysfunctional fate,

An empty broken dark life without a friend or a mate,

A degenerate filled with nothing but sorrow and guilt.

Now I can't even search for the stars, the sky it is filled
with an indefinable behemoth,

It surrounds me like a siege, it mocks my reality,

It has blurred my judgment, I cannot decipher
between right or wrong,

I am fading, decaying, fragile, a castle with glass walls.

I was a broken record, a silhouette of nothing.

Contagion

You are poison, one that is contagious,

You and your presence, you intoxicate my oesophagus,

Your eyes are a weapon of mass destruction,

 Every word they say is a volley of daggers,

You suffocate my soul, you are a leech,

You assimilate my synergy,

You are black magic, a curse set upon me,

A misfortune, a dilemma,

A misery I cannot forget nor live,

You are an enzyme; you break me down,

You are my depression, the reason I wear this frown,

You were my queen.

But now you are nowhere to be seen.

Ambigram

A faithful young lover, a rusty shield

An immature story for each other, a secret meeting in the field,

A promise to protect and shelter; A reunion that only time could meld and wield.

A saint by day, a sinner by night,

Sexing it by my say, cooking dinner by the fight,

Excuse me if I may, never mind just turn off my light,

Kissing and caressing you as I lay, praying that you get out of my sight.

My woman by morning, their whore by evening,

Lipstick on the mirror my god you look a darling,

Oh wait its dripping, must be my blood from wrist slitting,

Two inches left from the morgue, why are you scorning?

Love is what the world called it, just an ordinary married couple,

Love, six hours later a casket was lit, do you call this ordinary married trouble?

Exactly, no one gave a shit, another fatality, another dead lover.

How many will have to deal with this struggle?

Am I next?

Unfulfilled wish

I wish I could love you, but I do not know how to tell you.

I wish I could tell you all about it, but I cannot recall the past.

I wish I could just move on, but I am unable to forget the past.

I wish I could remove this sword from my heart like King Arthur'.

If only I could change the past and set my future with you.

If only I could show you the real me before all this happened.

Wish I could show you the edge of the earth and the brightest stars.

Wish I could make you mine and tell you all about my

scars.

Wish this all could happen so we could accept each other for who we are.

Wish I could refrain from my addictions,
Wish I could retrograde from the darkness,
Wish I could alternate the aftermath of my own actions.

But now it is too late because you are shinning in the sky.
Like a star. Oh, how I wonder what you are.
Oh, how I wish I could just say goodbye.

Empty

Look into my tormented eyes; stare into my empty soul,

Do not get startled it is not meant to be a surprise,

One minute I die a little, the next I smile,

I am here without you; I am shattered, and have been for a while,

See the truth that I have become,

Look into my enslaved heart, listen to the tale I am about to tell you,

You do not have to believe my word; just know it is my life

-and it is ending one memory at a time,

Who would have ever thought that love was a crime?

The fact is that a key is missing.

And my love is broken; it is the definition of drowning,

It has left me hopeless but still, I am here relentless,

I am trying to fly whilst barely lying lifelessly on the ground.

The fact is that;

You will never be mine, but I will forever be yours.

Kindest regards

I never thought it would have come to this,
I thought love was to be continued...

I always saw you as the foundation of my world,
The reason I was created, but now I am living to die, to
be cremated,
If only I could be relieved of this pain, pacified or
sedated,
I cannot believe I not only called you my wife but my
life,
I wish we formed our own fraternity,
A mini-me or a princess, who had your eyes,
I guess I was looking for all this in the wrong place,
Our love was a facade, a fake friend, a slap in my face,
My doubts were right, commitments always led to
disagreements and contradictions.
We always did fight, every moment an argument,
Every session with contraception,

Now I am left with all this guilt, trying to repress and
forget everything we built.
At least I know what love is and what it feels like.

It is a battle between good and evil, here evil has won.
It has left me with an eternity of pain, a constant
thumping at the heart and gone.
Every second it feels like a knockout blow to the heart,
a guillotine striking my hopes and dreams
leaving my heart as stone.

Never thought it would come to this,
I wanted to fulfil all your dreams and desires.
Make you a mother, provide for your father, and give
you everything I could acquire.

I thought love was to be continued...

Self-esteem

It was a difficult phase; a clash of emotions gripping my
heart and accompanying me,
I was fighting for survival and time was a luxury I could
not afford nor have,

In the beginning, it was a pleasantry with promise and
significance,
Soon though promises became rejection and
significance became unorthodox.

It was a war between me, myself and I try to sign my
death clause,
I was doing it for me, doing it for you, trying to accept
my own materialistic flaws,

It was a battle to gain my pride and retain my self-
righteousness and evade my everlasting anxiety,
I was dying thirstily for self-approval, to believe and
fully know I was worthy of you,

It was a pathetic fallacy of our love, a struggle, a tug of
war, on the verge of extinction,

I was my own scapegoat, sacrificing myself just so I could have a chance to be with you, a lover' scratch card,

You meant so much to me, that the feeling was unnatural,
A stomach full of butterflies, my confidence on the brink,
And my self-esteem was thinner than the tip of an icicle.
I even had thoughts of committing suicide.

This was my revolution, a tale of change, a lover's nightmare.

Vishwas

Looking back, the truth is that the road out of hell for
us was just too long,
We were young and immature, and everything was just
so wrong,
We wanted heaven but were dwelling in hell,
Our wishes were child's play and our love was illiterate,
With nothing set in stone and a fault in our stars.

As my teardrops fall to the ground, my heart sinks and
my feelings frown,
If only I still had your shoulder to cry on,
Then you would still have me to rely on, to pry upon,
I would still be your doll and you would be mine too.
So we could fix each other, be there to affix one
another,
Stay up late to convict the other,
Investigate and instigate another lie.

Perhaps you were right, this was the only option.
You were right in saying we lacked in Vishwas.
 Something I could not understand.

Looking back, in those days I could hardly stand,

But now I hear loud and clear, it is like a death wish, a battle cry,

That invigorates me If only I could turn back the time.

To earn your Vishwas.

It means trust. Our love was illiterate.

Will you?

When I'm gone you will miss me.

Say goodbye if you miss me.

But when I'm gone will you forgive me?

Will you love me? Will you cry for me?

Will you shed a tear for a memory of me?

Will you spend a penny of your time to think of me?

Will you spread out your hands like a butterfly and pray for me?

Will you have mercy on my faceless shadow and forgive me?

Will you miss me? Say goodbye if you miss me.

Will you forgive me? Say sorry if you forgive me.

Will you pray for me? Say amen if you prayed for me.

Will you love me?

Cursed

Cursed by a force I cannot outrun.
A king without a throne, it mocks my existence.
It manipulates my reality like an internet troll.
Is it Halloween already because it's always trick no
treat.
I'm constantly working over-time
 and rewarded with defeat.
The nights are getting darker and
my heart is still without a home.
I'm falling in love with those I can't have,
or they don't want me.
Am I destined for the morgue?
Because I know death won't reject me.
Or will it show love and kindness for its own pleasure,
Toying with my weakness, seasoning my wounds and
torturing what's left of me.

I put my soul on a mantle and admired it.
Reciting, dear friend you have suffered too much,
We must separate.
So naive I was, talking to myself again,
Because the one I knew was gone.

I befriend the vivid figure that stares back in the
mirror.

Maybe the morgue has accepted me as its own.

I put my soul on a mantle and admire it.

Dear friend you have suffered too much, we must
separate.

Reflections

Yesterday I was in a million pieces.

Today I am two less.

Two seconds from walking off a building complex.

My doctor says I'm getting better.

I believe we have different definitions of better.

Better at hiding my feelings.

I used to build walls higher than my house.

Now I live inside four of them.

What's the difference, what does it matter?

Last night I was holding on,

folding on my chances of success,

I've been drawing ever since I was in recess.

I know my ABCs like everyone single one of my ex's.

I've moved onto bigger things, better things.

Not seven inches, seven heavens.

I used to be a sinner, now I pray every Friday.

I used to be a saint, now I commit every day.

 I'm not perfect, I'm imperfectly perfect.

I tried to make a prayer but my sins are all I got.

I memorised a prayer but I forgot.

I used to sleep nine hours a day.

Now I sleep nine hours a night.

I'm embracing change like a cup of tea accepts milk.
All of my tomorrows can only be better than my
yesterdays.

Skeletons

I sleep with tears on my pillow.
They serve a memoir of the dreams,
I still need to kill off.
Without you they are empty, unfulfilled.
I have skeletons in my closet.
Remnants of dead whims,
You were never really there,
And never took time for me when you were.

I wonder why I still care.

Muse

She was a selfish eclipse, who refused to leave me
alone,
A clingy stalker, a degenerate who considered me to be
A friend, it was a despairs' ordeal she needed someone
to depend upon, she taught me to laugh through the
pain and how to search for my happiness,
All we had was each other, but she was a
schizophrenic,
She started forgetting the things she told me to
remember,
And starting remembering the things she told me to
forget.
And that is how I embraced the darkness,
It has always felt like home but it could just be an
elusive maneuver.
The sad part is I cannot even remember what it felt like
before each other.
It is just an array of blank spaces, I asked her and she
said to leave it a mystery like you.

Admittedly I am a narcissist who is his own inspiration.
The sad part it is the only truth I know, a truth of my
desperation.

Third person

You asked me to find my happiness.
The one sold in a bottle,
The artificial syrup you're meant to spit or swallow,
Or the ecstasy bullets that leave even more holes.
Couldn't you just be my poison?
It's no longer satisfying to stare into the hollow eyes
Of strangers and use them to fill the void of you, inside me.
We laugh out loud amplifying the emptiness, hoping tears will flow too.
They never do appear, they're absent from your presence.
Eventually, we end next to each other in search of happiness.

And the fucked up thing, you and I have to both accept.
It will never okay.
You will always be gone.
And I will never find my happiness.
Or that pair of arms that will hold you.
Smile and tell you it will all be okay.

Another round

You opened your arms,
Like the doors to heaven.
If only your eyes bared witness as such;
They burned agony, fear and a terrible past.
A smile appeared;
The type that would tame the devil himself,
Pity, the smile I spent my life trying to find.
I stared at the ground,
Burning a hole,
My world just splits into two.
I murmured, I've heard no pain no gain,
So what do I call you, the pain or the gain?
That smile appeared again.
Be my morphine she said,
Make my pain fade away.
Together we will sleep in peace.
And everything will be okay.

I leaned in and fell into her abyss,
I fell so deep.
I became her shadow.
I just didn't want to be alone.

Unrequited love

P-a-t-I-e-n-c-e
This was my love for you, I hoped you would let me.
Scrambled in my thoughts, lost in the moment.
I was not asking for your permission, just hoping
you would not stop me.
I tried my utmost best to stay away.
I just hoped that one day I would be able to forget you,
your face, your touch, the scent, all of it and you would
too.
But you are my apocalypse, the wind beneath my
wings,
the air I breathe and live.
Look in the tombs of my eyes and witness the reality,
the crypt that I have become,
the truth is we are a match forged in hell
you are my sentinel and I am your solace
I am cursed and so is my love for you
you are a silhouette that won't fade
and a memory I cannot erase.

This is my obsession and the story
behind my unrequited love for you.

I hated myself

I scream into the walls I'm home.

An echo asks was hell full?

What do you do when your environment is hostile?

What do you say when your presence is unwanted?

A rush of emotions encapsulates my breath space.

A blood clot expunges my humanity and I feel
alienated.

I curse my fortune; wish I could escape my fate.

Wish my mother's period was late.

OH the hate, how worse can it get?

When you despite your existence,

How much harm can comments from your mate do?

I remain speechless all the time but an alternative
voice

Screams fuck you.

It's ironic because that's what life says to me too.

Sad honest truth

A sad but honest truth, it no longer brings tears to my
eyes.
I've learned to embrace them with the pain and the
dawn breaking cries.
Once ordinary, I had dreams and a personality to be
adored.
A naive, I was giving my life to those who abused it, my
niceties were being whored.
The roses I planted turned into thorns and thistles.
Now they cast me with curses and whistles.
It transformed me into this insecure mess.
The end was near; I could feel the danger,
I had faced it before, only this time it was not a
stranger,
And I was not afraid, as I stood and stared at the
horizon
I saw nothing but a starless sky filled with nothing
But the mist of a storm, it was stunning.
I stood mesmerised as it rushed to swallow me whole.
I embraced the gushing as it thwarted me like a dead
soul.
They say what doesn't kill you makes you stronger.
I kissed death on the lips, and I fear death no longer.

I don't have time to explain

Would you believe that what we have been told about time is a lie?
It is an illusion. It is a false pretence.
It is a folk tale about demand and supply.
We let it settle and become complacent in the walls of our empty souls.
It is an intangible entity, an invisible language that we the use to control our lives.

Tell me, what would you if tomorrow it disappeared?
We are told that time heals everything.
Time is not a healer; it is a drug dealer,
It intoxicates our thoughts and keeps us company,
It infects our mind so we stay in touch,
We do everything in our power to attain more of it,
Misled is what we are, we drown in the desire for that getaway drug,
Time is a curse, a black magic set upon us, a misfortune we cannot escape.

<u>Losing myself</u>

I was left for dead, I was defenseless.

However, my mind it was relentless.

It was not willing to accept fate for what it was.

It was not going to play the hand that it was given.

My body was not ready to lie on the concrete to which

it was driven.

It was dark; it tore me apart like a ravenous beast.

My eyes were shields guarding me from against

contact.

My heart was a prison, trapping my anxiety and

frustrations.

It was emotional, a rollercoaster which almost took me

over the edge on many excursions.

If only I could tell you it would be easy.

I am here to tell you I made it, and I hope you do too.

From that day onwards, I was a drought; there was no

water under my bridge.

She looked into my eyes and pierced my heart like a

steak.

A phantom that said it was not good at goodbyes and

left in a whiff of the wind.

Shattered was my mirror of self-respect, along with all the hopes and dreams.

I miss you

I still remember it like it was yesterday,

You were laughing one second.

And you were gone the next.

Fate was casting our lives as a magic show.

If only life could rewind, so I could remind you,

How much you meant to me.

I still pray for you,

Plant flowers for you and grow tears for you.

But no flower will ever flourish the way you did or be able to replace you.

I miss you.

Soulless

When I am gone, will you miss me?
Say goodbye if you miss me?

Will you finally love me?
Will you let your tears cry for me?

Will you reminisce the memories of us?
Will you spend a penny of your time to think of me?
Will you spread out your hands
like a butterfly and pray for me?
Will you have mercy on my soul
and forgive me?

Alone

It's the key to evolution,

a ritual of rebirth, a chance to move on.

I've already served a life sentence;

I'd serve a lifetime of these.

Don't blame you for doubting me;

you're already looking at me like I'm on one.

Maybe I am, this is just the beginning.

Fuck it I'm high, find me on cloud nine,

I'm planting my feelings,

They're starting to grow on me, can't have that.

I'm forsaken, broken, I'm joking, and I'm taken.

See the point I'm making, they're suffocating.

I took my dreams and buried them 10 feet down,

and left a letter sorry I let you down.

I wanted love but it never wanted me.

Ironic, now it's running to me but I'm not interested.

It's a feeling I can't describe,

a pill they won't distribute or prescribe.

I was drunk, few too many tequila sunrises.

Trying to fill the invisible, to seduce the siege,

But it failed, they didn't understand me.

Nothing did.

I just had to accept that I was alone.

The Past

You are the blood in the cut,

I wasn't wise enough to confess,

What I felt, so I feel the pain it dealt.

I've heard it takes a moment to change a life,

I missed mine by an inch and a mile.

I would run a mile to have another one.

I only have a 9mm though.

I'm rebelling to survive,

Life isn't worth living if it's for no one.

I tried to live for myself but the feeling is numb.

So to the temptation, I will succumb.

Different

I'm chasing shadows in the sunlight.
I'm looking for light in the darkness.
I might be searching in the wrong places.
That's because I want to be different.

I want to be right in my own way.
I want to be the star in the day,
I want to shine radiantly in the night.

My dreams may not match yours.
We may not see eye to eye.
But that doesn't mean goodbye.

Life isn't always as simple as one equals one.
So let's accept each other's imperfections.
Before that opportunity too is gone.

The voices call

The voices call, screaming they saw me fall.

A premonition, that stands as a contradiction.

Because I stand tall, a flying skyscraper a shooting star,

I need this wish to come true,

So find me in the sky living stardust fantasies.

And on the newspaper showing universal love,

The headlines a pathetic fallacy of how I feel about you,

Still can't find the right words to say I love you.

You left a scar,

As you drifted away,

Now I find myself in an ocean, I'm drowning in emotion,

Searching for devotion, trying to be the one I wasn't,

I'm holding dearly onto yesterday and I'm falling into tomorrow

I can't keep living like this,

I'm a broken record.

Scratches stain the surface of my body.

I wear permanently like my second skin.

The nights I surrendered myself,

And the beating I took,

The torment of it all,
Taunts me to this day,
A haunted memory resides.
I'm a broken record.

I gave you everything I had,
Now there's nothing left to be said.

Judgement

My laugh its fake, a cover-up to look alive.
My posture's strong,
 So you ignore the scars I bear.
My happiness lies in a bottle
not liquor that's for the lonely.

I sit in a dark corner scared of death,
Yet you still stare at me.
The nights are eternal,
I need your hands to hold me,
Yet you point at me.
The emptiness is a hollow reality;
Your ignorance is a fatality.
You ignore me like a pebble in the sea,
 I'm drowning can't you see?

<u>Death anniversary</u>

Reminiscent, I took a walk to dead lover's lane.
It was that time of year again,
I had to pay tribute.
Gracious for the experience,
I watered my past.
I closed my eyes and let them bleed.
A monsoon of tears flowed,
I still needed the memory.
I could no longer let my wounds bleed,
I loved me too much.
I was never going back.
I had come a long way from suicide.
I promised myself I was always going to be there.
Nothing was going to take away the love
I gave myself.

Back to step one

Back to step one, where it all started,

Low self-esteem, broken heart and a vivid dream,

Tears falling on the page – look at my age,

Already drunk on vodka, wearing nothing but a khaki,

It's not mine but I'm fine with that, they took a heart
that wasn't theirs.

I'm topless but at least I'm unattached.

I turned my angels into demons and slew them all.

A lover went rogue, a renegade who's only fifteen.

Another razor blade went bloody, another day gone
empty,

I feel alone, the darkness hates me and the light burns
me.

I got blood on my lips and Ice in my fingertips.

Hate in my heartbeat but love on my mind.

I'm conflicted; it is pain to love you.

The reality is I can't live with you or without you.

The beatings are a ritual now, I call it making love.

Because I have to make myself believe you love me.

I'm delusional. Even hell becomes home once you've
settled in.

Four years

Four years and still counting, what happened to us?

Bonnie and Clyde, Romeo and Juliet –

Unfortunately, they died.

We are still alive and living, but in two different worlds,
we reside.

What happened to love in the air that has led us to bête
noir?

Who foresaw that our actions would lead to a crime
scene from LA Noire?

If you're reading this, then know that I too am
deceased like Curley's wife.

After all, I was only your plaything, hidden in the
shadows of your boudoir.

Today I am a shadow; they slit my tongue and left me
blind.

They are right, love is blind.

Love game

When did love and lilies become lust and lies?
What happened to 'til death do us apart, the kisses and
goodbyes.
I'm not expert but our generation has taken the love
out of sex.
Well, what's left, its dirt, a desperate attempt to feel
until one of us squirt?
Disconnected, disgusted. Not too sure what I expected,
as my body mourns,
It is suffocating to accept the truth; then again even
roses have thorns.

You saw love as a game, disappearing was your style,
An endless witch-hunt which waged heartbreak – it
was hostile.
I saw you as an opportunity to cherish, flourish and
love.
You saw it as a weakness, to shove words into my
throat.
I kissed you tenderly, too much to ask you though,
You only had one specialty - deep throat.

Tamed

It's tragic; you tamed the animal in me but killed the humanity in me.

You made my personality match your perfect description,

You transformed my life into a prescription, and you were its medicine,

It's humorous, you couldn't fulfil its role, and you were never much of a role model.

You span my world at the speed of light and stole the eye of my spirit animal.

Blinded my sight and made me lose the will to fight.

Moments of humanity linger, but your black magic eradicates time and time again.

When will it be enough for you? The commands, the pain...

They warned me about people like you.

You would stab me and disappear.

You would steal my honor and lead me to darkness.

Your memory it is a tremor, a hemorrhage amongst my cracks.

The sad part is that I gave you the permission to.

Reasons to laugh – I tell myself

Laugh to hold back the tears,
Laugh to overcome the fears of being judged for being weak,
Laugh to forget the love loss that occurred last week,
Laugh to fake a smile,
 Laugh to hide the fact you have been crying for a while,
Laugh to conceal the scars you bear,
Laugh to train your mind to see the good in everything,
Laugh to see the joy even when it hurts,
Laugh to hear the sound of hope even if it's temporary,
Laugh to feel,
Laugh to control,
Laugh to be.

Laugh.

Last night

I was done with running away from the past,

I was done with treating myself like an outcast,

It was time I removed my war paint and stopped
listening to sad songs,

It was time to sort my own life out that trying to fix
yours, to see right from the wrongs,

I had to look left even though it hurt because you
weren't treating me right,

I had to look for brighter horizons because I couldn't
live forever in this plight,

I had to fight, I had to struggle, I had to prepare,

I wanted to be ready; I wanted to be over, I wanted to
stop living in despair.

Progress

I know the price of success.

I've paid it to get so far.

I know the price of survival,

I've been there and got the scar.

I know the price of love; I've had my heart trapped in a jar.

I know the pain of heart-break; I've been a VIP in its 5-star bazaar.

I don't know the price of death,

But I've become its acquaintance; occasionally we bump into each other and spar.

I'm just saying I am not okay.

But I hope you are.

Seeking Salvation

Find me in the open,
amongst the sea beds
or in the middle of field.
The passion is unwinding.
How the wind takes me off my feet,
the open air rejuvenates my torn lungs,
Whistles of the wind charm my innocence
and I learn to fall in love again.

The sea rushes to embrace me,
its touch is unconditional,
relentlessly it attempts to appease,
and the purity of the waters infuses with
my delicate skin reliving me of my pain.
Endlessly the sea waves strengthening my spirit
and I learn what it means to be alive again.

Nature calls.
Will you answer?

<u>My story</u>

Wanderlust intoxicated the capsules of my veins
and the night swallowed me as I faded into its grasp.
 I emerged an angel on fire,
Holding hands with my lost courage.
The night almost conquered me,
as it teased death was an easy escape.
Even hell can look comforting if you're a cold bitch.

What's my story, read all about it,
the scars on my bare skin and
the footprints on my heart.
I'm not fully broken yet, falling apart but breathing.
About six breaths from depression again,
so I fell in love with the rain, they call me a pluviophile,
Together we cry when the whole world
looks down on me.
Everyone needs a home; my home
is wherever it's raining.

Frenemy

Once a best friend,
now that ship has come to a dead end.
I know I made promises, I've yet to keep.
And I've taken things, I've yet to return.
My life has taken my turn, now you're the third wheel.
Do you feel what I feel?

The feeling its karma, so stop rolling the dice.
You lied to me, said it was too late for the other side.
Well, look far it got you and the heights you reached,
and where it got me, I've descended into oblivion.
See, I don't even recognise myself,
And no one else does either.

You took me for granted,
had my feelings enchanted.
Well you're no longer the enchantress,
I'm taken.
So forget me.

Mohammed Ahmed

Sound of silence

Did you see my world has fallen?

You asked me to call your name.

Hear my screams, they still echo.

About an infinite amount of times, I called you.

The hells opened up,

thinking it was the day of judgement.

Roses lost their thorns for me but you are still nowhere

to be seen.

That sums up what I meant to you.

Grew up seeing you as my hero,

 I was just too blind to see past your disguise.

I find myself tangled in things that have nothing to do

with me.

But they are everything to do with you.

Hesitation

I only let certain people step into my life.
I have spent so long cleaning up my tears,
and blood I've lost trying to save others.

I've lost so much and gained so little.
I've grown so much yet been loved so little.
I've loved so much but have only been hated.
I've given so much yet the love I have received is
debated.

I've hesitated to fall ever since.
I've resisted to falling in love.
I've detested failure ever since.
Ironically, I've failed every attempt to heal ever since.

Stigma

Death is nothing at all.

Wake up to a game of Russian roulette.
Pills, bills, depression but none of it kills.
It hurts too much; you find it hard to breathe.
You starve; the medication kills your appetite.
Look in the mirror, you see bones.
Walk in to seek help, you're titled anorexic.
Tight clothes to hide the truth,
Face the eyes of a hundred men
wanting to uncover you.
You try to find the good, none.
The day passes and you are back to step one.
Living another day with depression.

Goodbyes don't have to be forever

Goodbyes don't have to be forever.
Unless you; want them to be.

It only takes one glint of a spark to
 rekindle the connection.
The sad part, only the courageous take the step.

I cried because you mattered,
the words you said I could not forget,
in fact, you never really left,
I carried your memory around like
I was divorced.
When the truth is we never started.

Apocalypse

I tried to move on.

But I stayed online when you went offline.

I said goodbye but I lied.

Addiction is an apocalypse.

Mine became finding happiness.

It was scarce and I thirsted for it.

I craved a drop of it.

I failed time and time again.

So I thought I'd find pain instead.

I almost found it in death.

Five years ago and counting,

I'm grateful for the light that saved me.

It renewed my sense and I can never repay its debt.

Wrong Advice

I exert all my energy
to attentively listen
to my devoted therapist,
I worshipped her advice.
I was naive,
she couldn't give a fuck.
Kept telling me I fucked up.
I was just another name she needed to tick.
She did make something click.
I vowed to never turn for another session.
Only when I healed, that was an exception.

I distanced myself from everyone around me.
Friends, family, everything I loved.
And gradually, I saw progress.
There were no bloodshot eyes.
No thoughts of suicide.

All I needed was space.
I just wish someone had told me earlier.

Mohammed Ahmed

Living Room

Everybody in the living room
this is where I used to be
standing in the dark
letting madness take over.
And you told me this was forever.

Look through the glass,
see the bunnies, and the butterflies,
they took me to the other side.
I inhaled the strawberry spring
and locked away this darkness in a place called my
past.

Found therapy in peace.
Counting seconds and living life in minutes.
Tomorrow will be different.
A jouska, I repeat the chorus.
I learned to cuddle my scars and kiss a few.

I found therapy in peace and solace in darkness.
Counting in seconds and living in minutes,

harnessing memories I vowed to forget.
Learning to cuddle my own scars
and kissing a few at a time.

Nobody understood me, I was lost.
So I faced it alone.
Found myself by standing in the dark,
I faced my fears and stand tall conquering the worst of
them.

THANK YOU FOR BEING A PART OF MY STORY.
I AM GRATEFUL TO MY INSTAGRAM FOLLOWERS,
IF YOU ARE READING THIS BOOK OR HAVE READ
MY PIECES.

I WAS ALWAYS AFRAID AND FELT I WAS ALONE.
THANK YOU FOR HELPING ME OPEN UP AND
HEAL. THANK YOU FOR BEING THERE.

MOHAMMED AHMED
@STYLE_POET

A POEM FOR EACH AND EVERY ONE OF YOU.

Just want to say thanks.
You made me feel beautiful when I was broken and
lost.
You made me feel when the only thing I felt was numb.
You made me feel like I didn't need the world's
approval.
You were my connection when I was disconnected.
You were my world when all else collapsed.

If there is one person in the world who wishes you the
best in the world, it's me.

Mohammed Ahmed

36275506R00060

Printed in Great Britain
by Amazon